MW00514260

The Wise Words of
Spot Beaglemore

The Words, Wit & Wisdom
of Spot Beaglemore

- American Philosopher
- Poet
- TV Gag Writer

the Peppertree Press
Sarasota, Florida

For information regarding permission,
call 941-922-2662 or contact us at our website:
www.peppertreepublishing.com or write to:
the Peppertree Press, LLC.
Attention: Publisher
1269 First Street, Suite 7
Sarasota, Florida 34236

ISBN:978-1-936051-07-6

Library of Congress Number: 2009925090

Printed in China

Printed April 2009

This book is dedicated to Connie Pace, a woman of faith, for teaching me that wishes do come true.

Marvin for taking all the pictures and writing down all my words.

Sara Mantle for putting it all together.

Preface

I have written this book with the hope that some of the human beings that I share this planet with will find a smile, some insight on what we non-humans think (Yes we do think) and perhaps a philosophical thought or two that may enrich your life.

Spot Beaglemore

Contents

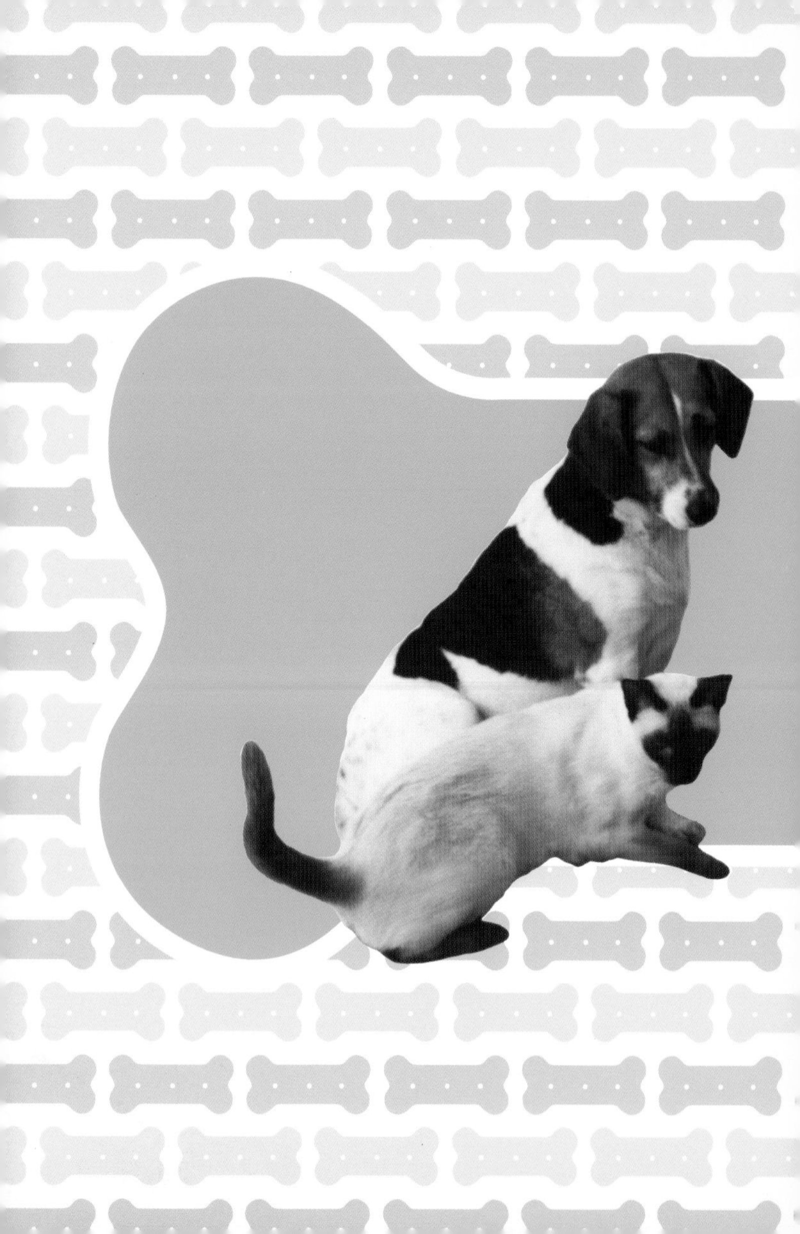

Part One:

My Observations and Thoughts

A warm shelter,
A good meal,
A pat on the head and

A long walk from
time to time.

Don't knock
the
dog's
life.

SPOT

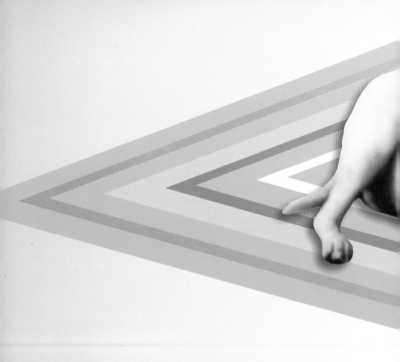

A warm pool of sunlight,
A soft wool rug,
The anticipation of love
When the comfort of her voice
Is heard from the kitchen

— **Happiness**
is then complete.

Love is one's **reward** for being a **good dog.**

Sharing
is the
first step

to understanding
the law of abundance.

The world possesses endless abundance, enough for all of the needs of all of God's creatures. While here on earth, we are permitted to share in and be the caretaker for this bounty. We never really own any of it. By sharing that which finds its way into your care you open the door to the treasure house of the world.

Logic

has **no** validity in an **illogical** world.

When the world accepts that which is real and discards the false values that have caused war and suffering throughout the ages, then will reason prevail.

The
thirst
for
knowledge
is best quenched
by an active **curiosity**.

Optimism

is the one

essential
ingredient

in what ever

is cooking.

23

Communication

is the

greatest

artistic

endeavor.

The poet, the artist, musician and the philosopher are only concerned with making a statement. If this is done it is truly a work of art.

Greatness
begins
with
great
heroes.

There is more beauty in the **written word** than there is in a **T-bone steak.**

The best things that you
can give your children are

Love,
Understanding
and Freedom.

A few bones in the bank
wouldn't hurt either.

Riches are fine

but not worth the price

if you don't
take time to

stop and

smell

the
trees.

Do not gossip.

Carry no tails except your own.

A friend is a **treasure –** share him with the **world.**

Let the world see your example that a true friendship is worth working hard to attain and keep.

Do not judge
your friends
with another's eye.

Death is birth on another plane.

Birth brings with it resistance, fear and the desire to remain in the secure world of the known. Birth is the death of life in the womb. Why should we doubt that life as we know it is merely another step in the evolution of eternal life.

Children are the expression of
your confidence in immortality.

**Not your immortality
but the world's.**

Take a lot
of time to

think.

Take more time
before you

speak.

I've done a lot of car chasing in my days

but very little thought of what I would do if I ever caught one.

Good Luck

without understanding

is better than

Bad Luck

without understanding.

Think about it.

Joyce Kilmer was the **victim** of a **wrong audience.**

Think about it.

Now I lay me
down to sleep.

It's 11 o'clock.

Do you know where your kids are?

Part Two:

Some of My Poetry

The shadows lengthened to form the silhouettes of jungle beasts and imagination creates a place of fear.

The noise of the wind sings a wailing song of terror and the coming night hides the faces of the unknown.

Then comes the reassuring voice of love and a hand of confidence strokes my back and all is well again.

I sometimes walk the crowded street
In search of friendly faces.
And marvel at the smiles I meet
In most unusual places.

The ones who take the time to stop
And share a moment's pleasure
Are in my mind the very top
Of all of life's great treasure.

My sad eyes belying my wagging tail
As I sense he's near.
"Here boy," he says as he walks through the door
And I fly down the stairs.

I waited so long for him to return
He said he had things to do.
But it's unfair to be alone so long
To sit alone and stew.

Look deep into sanguine pools or strain
to see below the crust of angry seas,
or stare beyond the stars where heaven
ought to be –
        all to no avail.
You'll never know the end of God's mystery.

In the spring when birth abounds and hope
gathered from sleeping dreams
sounds the alarm to bring anew,
we too will hear and wake to life
to fulfill our part of destiny.

68

October 1ˢᵗ

In the dead of the night the artist
came and color flowed to his brush
from a magic palette.
And when I awoke at the dawn
of the day –
      I beheld October.

Thanksgiving

The colors so vivid that you can
inhale the fragrance,
The taste of burning wood,
The touch of frost upon your cheek,
The sense of eternity beyond knowing
As the leaves fall willingly and unafraid.

City streets
lurking -- yielding
strange faces
any time of night.
traffic noises
never stopping
don't these people ever sleep?
Torn up streets
mass confusion.
Is all this real
or just illusion?
Like broken promises we never keep.

Sunflower

Fragile giant
    with bold yellow face

Surveying the earth
    from lofty heights,

Swaying rhythmically
    at the slightest breeze

Praying to the same Creator.

Pigeons

The national bird of the city park –
dull grey feathers,
dull grey mind
searching for food their constant chore;
staying alive
just staying alive.

Every so often thoughts of romance
begin to invade
their dull grey minds,
they must continue to create their kind.
They must survive.
Why, tell me why?

Nothing new
    to say today.

Think I'll take
    a **biscuit break.**

Sometimes I doodle a little too.